The Whompa Whompa Whompa Germs!

By: Julie Neathery

Illustrated By: Steve Meredith
Graphic Design by: Rick Neathery

ALL RIGHTS RESERVED: No part of this publication may be reproduced, stored in a retrieval system, or transmitted in any form or by any means – electronic, mechanical, photocopy, recording, or any other – except for brief quotations in printed reviews, without the prior permission of the author.

ISBN: 978-1-64288-140-0

Copyright 2020 by Julie Neathery
Published by Derek Press
Cleveland, TN 37311

Printed in the United States of America

I dedicate this book to:

*My Lord and Savior, Jesus Christ,
thank you for your inspiration and your infinite grace!
My husband, Rick, thank you for your love,
support, and encouragement. I love you!
My daughters, Felicia, Jessica, and Bethany,
I love each of you so very much.
My grandchildren, always remember,
Nona loves you, but Jesus loves you more!*

One very cold winter morning, Kinzy went with her cousin, and best friend, Gage to the hospital to have an operation because Gage was sick. Uncle Tim and Aunt Bette, who were Gage's mommy and daddy, had to take them because Kinzy and Gage were both only two years old. They could not go to the hospital by themselves.

After arriving at the hospital, Gage had to go to the operating room. Kinzy was sad because she could not go with him. She had to stay in the waiting room with her Pappy and Nona and the rest of the family until Gage's operation was finished.

Have you ever had to go to the hospital because you were sick?

While in the waiting room, everyone was sitting around together talking and reading books. Kinzy's brother, Kaleb, asked if they could play with their toys. As soon as Kinzy sat down by her Nona, she took her shoes off and started to get down from her chair to walk and play on the floor.

"Oh no Kinzy", said Nona, "You must put your shoes back on! You cannot walk around in this hospital without shoes on your feet."

With her eyes opened wide, Kinzy looked up and said, "Please Nona?"

"No shoes, no shoes" said Kinzy "I don't like shoes!"

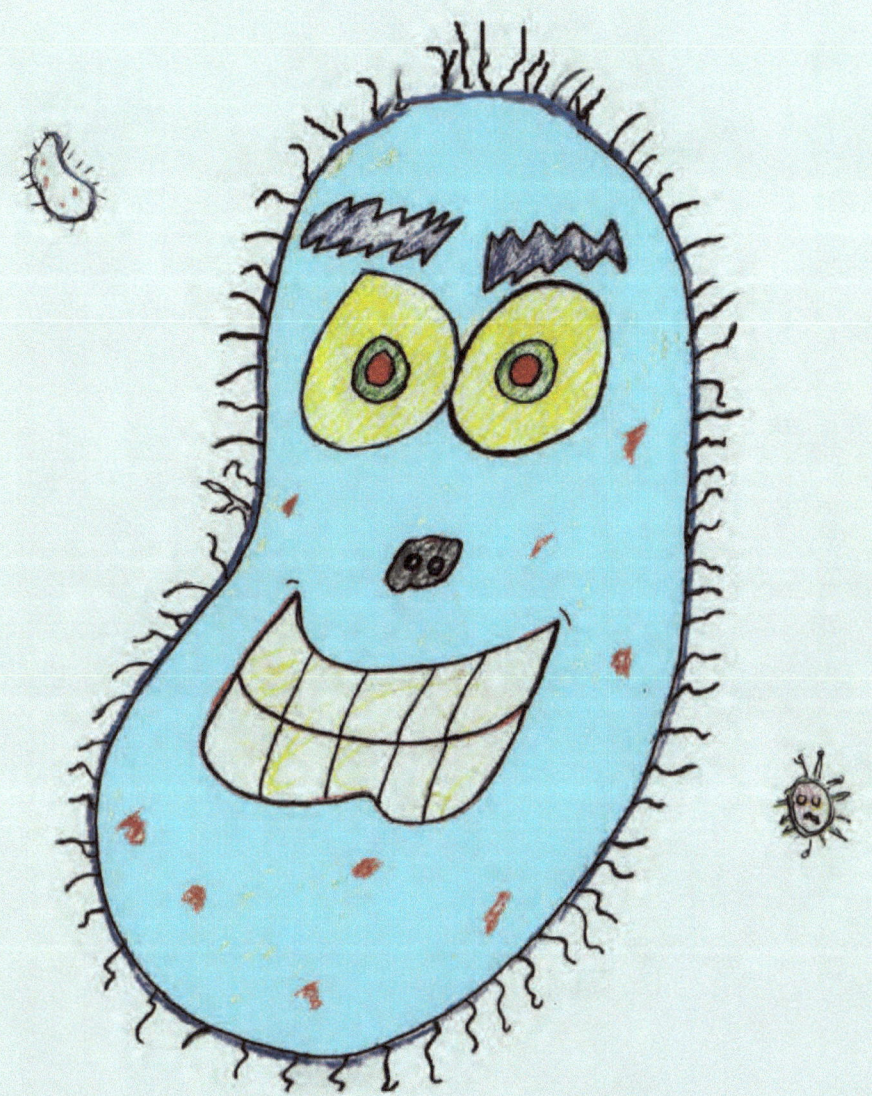

"Kinzy, baby girl, if you walk around in here without your shoes on, you will get the whompa, whompa, whompa germs! And you do not want the whompa, whompa, whompa germs!"

Kinzy looked at her Nona with her big brown eyes, she crinkled up her little nose, and asked; "Whompa, whompa, whompa germs; what is that?" She then looked down from her chair at the floor and said, "I don't see them. Where are they?"

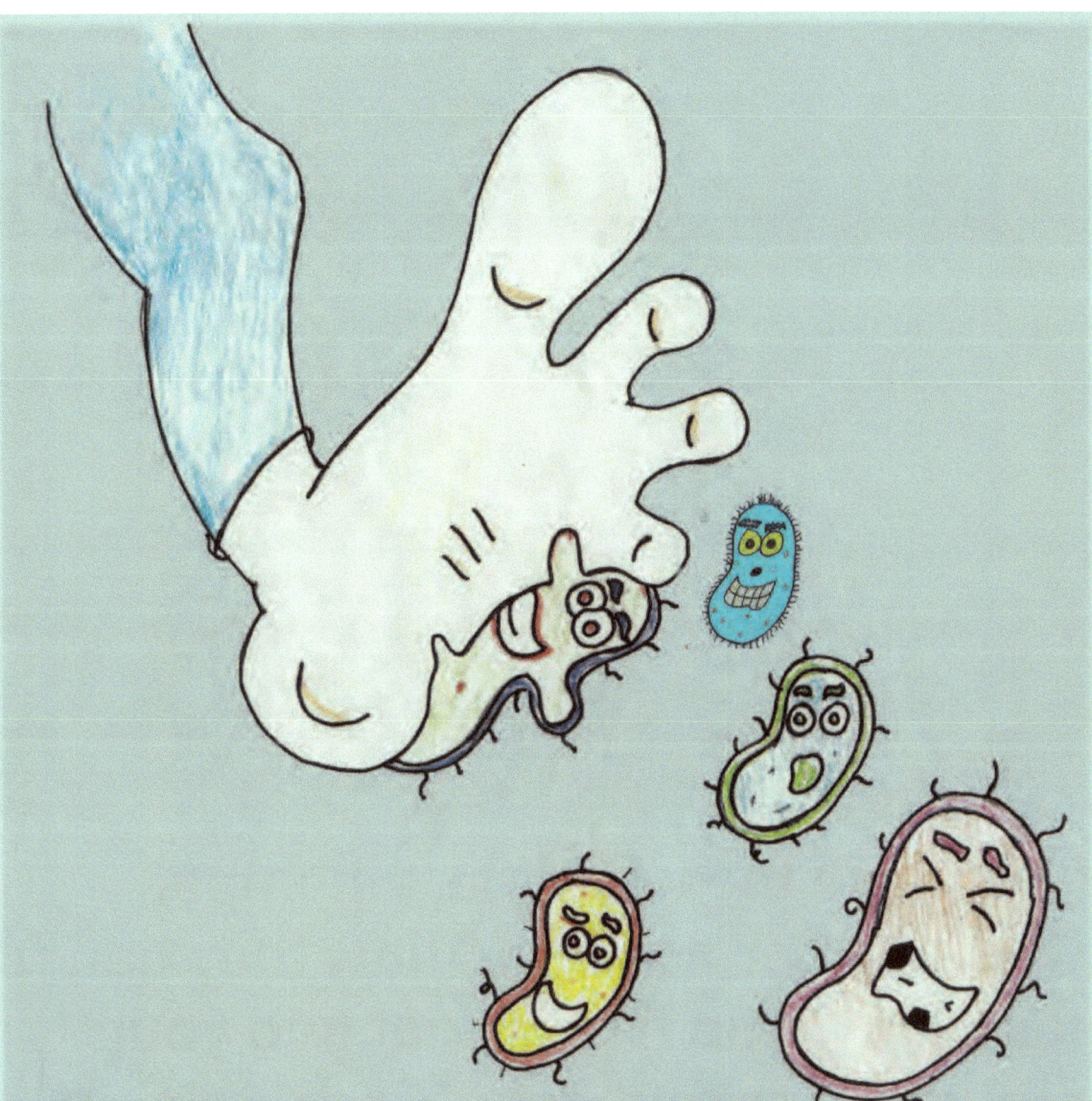

"No, you cannot see them with your eyes, but they are there", said Nona. "They are very, very tiny, but they will make you sick. They will get on the bottom of your feet when you walk."

Have you ever seen any whompa, whompa, whompa germs?

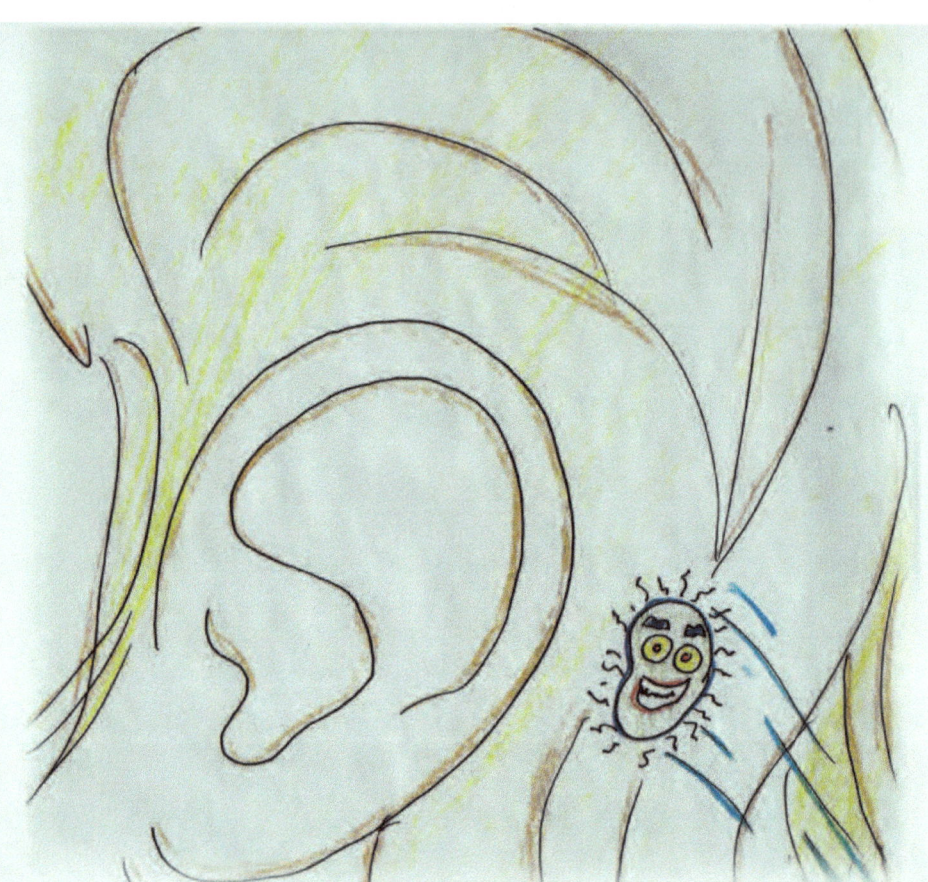

"Because the whompa, whompa, whompa germs are so tiny, they can run fast, and jump high to get into your mouth, ears, and nose. The whompa, whompa, whompa germs want to make everybody sick. That is why you must wear your shoes, cover your mouth when you cough, and always wash your hands!"

Do you wash your hands?

Nona then looked away from Kinzy; but she could still see her out of the corner of her eye. Without saying a word, Kinzy scooted over very quickly in her chair, picked up her shoes, and put them back on her feet.

"Kinzy! I am so proud of you. You put your shoes on!" Kinzy looked at Nona, crinkled up her nose, and shook her head back and forth very slowly and said,

"I don't want the whompa, whompa, whompa germs Nona!"

She jumped down from the chair and started playing with her toys. She was safe from the whompa, whompa, whompa germs because she had her shoes on.

The End